Endurance, Enrichment, & Encouragement

ALYSSA MOORE

I want to thank my mother, Lynette Rivers, my grandmother Eliza Rivers, and my grandfather Alphonse Rivers, but most of all, my deceased father, Rickey Moore. Mom, you are a strong woman to have picked up the slack, and I thank you for it.
To my grandparents, thank you for raising me to be the woman that I am today. Thank you for teaching me the ins and outs of life, and thank you for always being there for me on good days and bad. Thank you for helping me.
Dad, thank you for always being by my side, whether right or wrong.
Thank you all for supporting me in everything that I do.
I love you'll!

Chapter One

"Girls look at boys as accessories. Boys look at girls as necessities." - Pastor R.C. Blakes

I will never forget the walk to the Dean's office. I felt my heartbeat all over my body. Beads of sweat formed on my forehead as my eyes nervously bounced around. The long hallway seemed never-ending and particularly cold for such a humid New Orleans day.

I was in my sophomore year of undergrad at Xavier University when I was told that the Dean wanted to see me. I had no clue why. I hoped that there was no bad news, but something felt off.

"Good afternoon, Miss Moore," the Dean said, "Please have a seat."

"Good afternoon, Dean. Thank you." I stumbled over my words.

I glanced around her office at family photos that were in beautiful picture frames.

She wasted no time with pleasantries. She got straight to the point.

"Miss Moore, the reason I have you in my office today is that your grades are not up to par. Because of last semester's grades, your music scholarship has been pulled. To continue this semester, you will have to pay your tuition out of pocket."

My heart sank and a lump formed in my throat. Where was I going to get thirty thousand dollars from and before Monday? Tears streamed down my face, and my head spun.

I asked the Dean if there were any other options to stay enrolled at Xavier.

She advised that I could enroll in a nearby two-year college, get my grades in good standing, then transfer back to Xavier.

At that moment, I gave up on college. Don't get me wrong; I understood that it was all my fault. But I was so hurt. I felt that I'd let down the people who mattered the most. How would I break the news to them?

I cried the entire ride home. I couldn't imagine the look of disappointment I would soon face. As soon as I arrived home, I told my mom and grandmother that I needed to talk to them. Through tears, I laid everything out on the table. My mother's words rang in my ears.

"If you'd put Alyssa first, you wouldn't be in this predicament."

My grandmother wasn't so subtle. She shouted, "You lost a fourteen thousand dollar music scholarship and wasted a loan that your mother took out for you? How inconsiderate and selfish can you be?"

I held my head low in shame. I hated disappointing the matriarchs of my family. They've always been so supportive of me.

. . .

As if things couldn't get any worse, I was having an awful day at work. At the time, I worked at a major retail chain. I didn't hate the job, but it wasn't my dream job. A co-worker gave me a task that wasn't in my job description. I knew that it was something that she didn't want to do, so she volunteered me without my consent.

Another co-worker who was a work friend noticed the frustration on my face. She secretly texted to ask me what was wrong. I responded, "This bitch got me fucked up. I wanna stab her." Now, in no way did I mean that literally. I was upset and venting. And besides, I was talking to my homegirl, not my manager. There was no harm in that. I got through that working day and exhaled as soon as I clocked out.

On Sunday, as I attempted to clock into work, my supervisor stopped me.

"Alyssa, they need you in the back office."

When I entered the back office, there were people in business suits that I'd never seen before. I assumed they were upper management. Everyone who worked in the store dressed casually. I sat in the office chair and asked if I were in trouble.

"Miss Moore, we have a text message from an associate of you threatening another associate."

I immediately knew what he was talking about. But my homegirl couldn't have told on me, right?

He showed me a piece of paper that had a copy of the text exchange magnified on it.

"Is this your phone number," he asked.

"I didn't mean that, though. I said it out of anger," I looked around the room at the member of upper management, "Haven't you guys ever said anything out of anger?"

Each face had the same poker face. The only emotion in the room came from me. I knew I'd lost my job.

"Miss Moore, it is a violation of store policy."

He went on to tell me that I was being let go and would

not be eligible to work at any stores or affiliated stores of the mega-chain in the future. I could have screamed, but I exited politely. I held my head up until I gathered my belongings and sat in my car. Then, I broke down with a waterfall of tears.

How much more could I take?

I had another disappointment to tell my family, and I wasn't looking forward to it.

As I poured my heart out to my grandmother, my phone rang. I saw that it was my pain-in-the-ass boyfriend, so I declined the call. I didn't want to be rude to my elders. The phone rang another two times before my grandmother's phone rang. She answered.

"Who is this," she asked.

"Grandma, I was drunk, and I went down a one-way street. The car is totaled. I'm scared that they are going to take me to jail because Alyssa took the insurance and registration paperwork out of the car."

She turned to me and asked about the paperwork. I told her that it was at my mom's house. So, we got in the car to retrieve the papers. My grandmother spoke with the police over the phone. I believe that her sweet heart and spirit touched the police officer and probably saved Roy from an absolute nightmare.

How did I get in this place in my life? Nothing was going right. I started questioning everything, and Roy was number one on the list.

Chapter Two

"You don't want a 'Build A Bear' a person that you have to teach how to be a man." - Pastor R.C. Blakes

On March 16, 2014, I met a guy named Roy on Facebook. He didn't approach me like other guys who slid in my DM did. Roy seemed different, and I was intrigued. He messaged me and said that I was beautiful, he'd love to get to know me, and left the ball in my court by attaching his cell number. We instantly hit it off, and it wasn't long before he asked me out to the movies for our first date.

I picked him up. When he came outside, I was relieved that he was better looking than I assumed. I didn't think there would be a physical attraction, but when I saw him, I felt a spark. My first mistake was letting the first red flag slide. As I drove to the theatre, Roy received a text message from who he claimed was his play sister. I should have trusted my gut. He called her on the phone and told her that he was now in a relationship and could no longer play brother and sister with her. I ate it up and blushed the remainder of the ride.

Our romance intensified quickly. When he told me that he loved me, I was on top of the world. The next step was for him to meet my parents. We were moving fast. My family welcomes everyone. They have pure hearts. I almost teared up when my grandfather gave Roy his phone number. My grandfather jokingly told him that I could be a handful at times, and if Roy ever needed him, he was only a phone call away.

From then on, Roy became a fan of my grandmother's cooking. He was around for Sunday dinners or whenever my grandmother cooked. When he came around, he played ball with my little sister; Roy had become a part of the family.

Months went by, and my family accepted Roy as a part of the family. He was around so much that he started coming to church with us. After church, my grandmother would always take us to a breakfast spot. Our Sundays became routine.

We usually met at Burger King on Canal Street when I got out of school around 3:15 PM. It was always the highlight of my day. After school, we decided to go to his mother's house, which wasn't far from Burger King. After Roy checked the mailbox, his entire mood changed. The sudden shift concerned me. He sat me down and looked into my eyes before telling me the letter's information. I immediately grew erratic and stood to leave. Hearing the commotion, his niece and mother came into the room.

"Why didn't you tell me that you had a child," I shouted.

In a calm tone, his niece responded, "Alyssa, that's not his baby. She's only doing this because Roy isn't taking care of her baby anymore."

I was stunned. Her words echoed in slow motion.

His niece continued, "Roy took care of her son when they were together. But, unfortunately, her baby's father is in jail."

Roy chimed in by saying that he signed his name on the

birth certificate, thinking that having a father figure would give the baby an advantage. But now, he was being sued for child support. Nevertheless, Roy stepping up to the plate was admirable, and I decided at that moment that I would stick by his side.

The following day was my orientation to Xavier University of Louisiana. I wasn't in the suitable headspace to absorb all of the information given at orientation. Instead, my mind was wrapped around Roy and how I could help him. When we broke for lunch, instead of networking with the other enrolling freshman, I found a quiet spot to do research and make a phone call.

"Thank you for calling New Orleans Bar Association. How may I help you?"

I asked the young receptionist if any available lawyers handled child support cases.

She located a local lawyer and gave me the contact information. When there was no answer at the firm, my heart sank. I felt like giving up because Roy was against a deadline to respond to the court paperwork. I had to help my boyfriend. I left a voicemail and prayed that I'd receive a call back soon.

Two days later, my prayer was answered.

"Hi, this is Lindsay from New Orleans Bar Association. Am I speaking with Ms. Moore?"

I was so excited to get the help Roy needed finally. I explained the situation to Lindsay. She told me she could take the case with a five hundred dollar retainer. I knew Roy didn't have the money because he'd just started a new position at Walmart.

As soon as I got paid, I purchased a money order to retain legal representation for Roy. I immediately gave her the $500 via money order soon as I got born from Walmart. Stressed and worried, I finally confided in my grandmother and told her what was happening. She told me not to worry and gave her the lawyer's information. She told me that she would contact the attorney and handle everything. My grandmother immediately spoke with Lindsay and introduced herself. She advised Lindsay to contact her if there were any updates to the case. My grandmother saved the day. I felt the stress lift from my shoulders.

After three weeks, the attorney contacted my grandmother with news that she'd located the baby's mother. The woman agreed to a blood test. I was anxious to get the results and put the whole ordeal behind us. I felt like the trial would make our relationship stronger.

I accompanied Roy to the lab to test his DNA, and after three weeks, we heard from Lindsay again. We finally had a trial date, but the results were in before we could go to trial. Roy was proved not to be the father. I couldn't wait to go to trial and put this behind us.

On the day of the trial, I had an uneasy feeling in my stomach. I knew that we didn't have anything to worry about. The proof was in the DNA, but I was anxious for it all to be over. My grandmother accompanied Roy and me to trial. The baby's mother wasn't present in court, but she sent a long letter to Ms. Lindsay apologizing for wasting Roy's time. The attorney presented the letter to the judge and dismissed Roy's case. The icing on the cake was Ms. Lindsay informing my grandmother that the case was easy and that we didn't owe anything outside of the five hundred dollars we'd paid. I thanked God that justice was served as we left court that day.

Chapter Three

"Never satisfy a man who can't give back the same energy." -
Pastor R.C. Blakes

In April of 2017, Roy and I decided to get an apartment together. I paid the deposit and the first month's rent because Roy didn't have the money at the time. However, before we received the keys, I laid down the law. There were stories of Roy's brother Brandon. He has mental issues and should've been under supervised care. I explained to Roy that his brother would not be able to live with us by any means. I didn't feel safe with him around.

Roy pretended to respect my boundary but countered with, "Eventually, my brother is going to have to stay with us because he has nowhere to go."

His words made the hairs on the back of my neck stand up. I didn't have the strength to argue with Roy, so I told him that I understood. I was still apprehensive.

It wasn't long before things started going downhill with Roy. Our arguments became routine, and most of the time, I couldn't remember where our arguments stemmed from.

One evening, I chatted with him as I drove home from work. Unfortunately, our conversation turned into an argument, and Roy had the nerve to tell me that he should've gotten back with his ex so they could be a family with her son. I couldn't believe he dared to say those words to me. They were beyond hurtful. After all, I had done for him, he made me feel like it wasn't enough. I'd become accustomed to Roy saying nasty things to get a reaction out of me, but this was disrespectful.

When I arrived home, I wasn't thinking straight. After throwing my purse on the couch, I went into the kitchen and retrieved the biggest knife I owned. I trotted up the townhouse stairs and entered the room where he was.

"Bitch, what did you say?"

I stuck the knife in his direction so he could see it in my hand. Roy knocked the knife from my hand, and we wrestled until we were both out of breath. After we separated, Roy called my grandmother to tell me like I was a little kid. I was infuriated.

Roy and I had reached the point of no return. Things got out of hand fast, and it was scary. He left and took all of his clothes. I sobbed as my grandmother helped me gather my belongings. Finally, I decided that it would be best to move back in with her.

The next day, I gave the apartment complex thirty days' notice that I would be moving. I was heartbroken. Roy and I only shared space for two months.

Back at my grandparent's home, I hoped to recover from Roy. I was working on purging him from my system when I received a phone call from him. His mother had died. I was devastated. And, just like that, Roy and I were back on again.

A few months went by, and we decided to try living together again. I did all of the research, put the deposit down, and we moved in quickly.

Things were going great until I received a phone call from the apartment office that I had a prorated rent-charge of four hundred dollars because we moved in in the middle of the month. My mind started racing. I had no idea how I would come up with the money. I only had one hundred dollars. I need three hundred more. Because my name was on the lease, I paid the deposit and purchased the apartment furniture; I figured it wouldn't be a big deal for Roy to pay the remaining balance.

When I presented Roy with the predicament, he gave me an attitude. I couldn't believe his audacity. He gave me three hundred dollars, and I paid one hundred dollars to the apartment office. Though we were over another hurdle, his attitude didn't sit well with me.

The next day when he got off work, he told me that we needed to talk. He mentioned that his brother was on the street and had nowhere to go. Then, he gave me an ultimatum. He told me that he was leaving if his brother couldn't live with us. I loved Roy so much that I was willing to sacrifice my comfort if it made him happy.

Roy had an issue with his brother contributing anything to the household. His brother received government assistance, and Roy had a problem with using some of the assistance to put groceries in the house. I carried most of the household load; buying groceries was the least his brother could do. I was fed up.

Our arguments had become so routine that half the time, I didn't know what we were arguing about while we were arguing. Then, Roy called me a bitch in one argument that triggered me. I didn't deserve the disrespect. I had been good to

Roy and suppressed my happiness for him. I made him my priority, and I'd had enough.

I told him to pack his stuff and his brother's belongings and leave. I reminded him that I'd purchased everything in the apartment and he should only go with his and his brother's clothes. I was done with Roy.

Chapter Four

"You don't have to buy love." - Pastor R.C. Blakes

W e've all heard the saying, *The best way to get over one man is the attention of another.* The same day that Roy and I broke up, I called Ruben to come over to my apartment. I told him that he could move in with me now that Roy was gone. Ruben and I met two weeks prior when my friend Angelica and her boyfriend Damien introduced us. We all became fast friends and started hanging out regularly. I ignored all of Roy's calls. Someone new had my attention, and I enjoyed Ruben's company. My friends thought that Ruben would be perfect for me. Damien campaigned for Ruben before I met him. He shared that Ruben would treat me like a queen and provide. Those were two things that I didn't receive with Roy, so I was excited to meet this mystery man.

I invited Ruben over to my place for movie night. As we watched the film, he made a promise to always protect and provide for me. The red flag should've been that Ruben was just released from jail and didn't have a job.

I allowed him to move in, and he soon asked if his brother could move in. My first thought was, *here we go again with another brother,* but I cared about Ruben, so I agreed. At the time, I worked two jobs. I've always been a go-getter, which is one of the things I believe attracted men to me. So I held myself down and picked up their weight too.

My grandparents weren't fond of my new arrangement. They took me off of their car insurance, and I felt sick. When I finally got the nerve to ask my grandmother about me being dropped, she didn't hesitate.

"You have a man who doesn't do shit for you, yet you reward him by letting him drive your car. He doesn't even put gas in your car."

I became defensive and told her that Ruben had put gas in my car. It was a lie that I hoped she believed, but my grandmother knew better.

I was off on Sundays. It became the day that Ruben, Angelica, Damien, and I hung out. We'd grab a bite to eat or check out a local hangout. I got comfortable with my new crew and felt comfortable letting them use my car. They used to tell me that I worked so much that I deserved to be driven around. Ruben's brother never hung out with us because of his work schedule. My grandmother would say that I was being used. I didn't feel that way, though.

One evening, one of Ruben's friends sent him an article that stated a warrant for Ruben's arrest. He was wanted for aggravated assault. I was more upset and hurt than Ruben was. I asked him what his plan was. Ruben stated that he didn't have one. He had no plan of turning himself in because he claimed he was innocent. I cried myself to sleep that night from worry.

The next day, I mentioned Ruben's warrant to my aunt.

Her advice was for me to get Ruben out of my apartment. She told me that I could be arrested for harboring a fugitive. I was scared.

That night, Angelica, Damien. Ruben and I strolled down Bourbon Street. We purchased a few cocktails and tried to get my mind off of Ruben's warrant. Unfortunately, I broke down in tears in the middle of Bourbon Street. We decided that it was best if we called it a night.

Angelica lived next to me. When we all said our goodbyes and were home, Ruben informed me that he had decided to turn himself in.

The next night, I accompanied Ruben to the police station and watched as he told an officer that he was there to turn himself in. Tears formed in my eyes as I watched him be hand-cuffed and taken out of sight.

I cried and screamed for Ruben as he was taken away. Finally, he turned around and told me that he would be okay and loved me. After that night, I fell into depression. I didn't want to talk to anyone, not even my friend and neighbor Angelica.

I started to feel as if Angelica was getting way too comfort-able using my car. They didn't even put gas in it. Once Ruben was inside, I didn't want to be bothered. When she asked to use my car, I flat out told her no with no explanation.

Angelica didn't like me pulling away. She started knocking on my door frequently. Ruben's brother still lived with me. I used to tell him not to answer the door because I knew it was her. One day, Angelica got bold. She banged on the door repeatedly. It seemed as if the banging got louder and louder. Finally, I couldn't take it anymore. I stomped to my front door and ripped it open.

"WHAT DO YOU WANT?"

In a calm tone, Angelica asked, "So, you not fucking with us anymore?"

"No, I'm not. I'm staying to myself. I'm good."

She stomped away, and I thought it was over, but I was wrong.

The following day, I received a phone call from someone telling me to check on my car because Angelica had flattened one of my tires. I knew that if I were to go outside that it was possible that Angelica and I would get into a physical altercation, so I decided to call the police to report the crime. If I would've stepped out of my door, I know that I would've lost my freedom. My temper would take over. I had too much to lose. But, unfortunately, the police only came out and made a report that wasn't any help to me.

It wasn't long before I became burned out trying to help Ruben. His phone calls were adding up fast. They were expensive. I started to take out payday loans to provide what he needed while behind bars. The loans started to accumulate, and I was in over my head. I'd transferred to Delgado Community College and was expecting a refund check. I planned to move away from the city. Ruben's brother helped find a lovely two-bedroom rental home. He gave me two hundred dollars towards the house, and we were moved in weeks.

Ruben being behind bars was extremely expensive, and I missed him. So with my next refund check, I planned to bring my man home.

I talked to Ruben's brother about signing him out of jail if I paid his bond. I wasn't old enough to do so on my own. The next day, we went to a bail bondsman. I was one step closer to having Ruben in my arms. The bail bondsman was a sweet lady who reminded me of my grandmother. She talked to me as if I were one of her precious grandchildren. She explained the process to me and Ruben's brother. Ruben's bond was ten percent of twenty thousand dollars was two thousand dollars, but I didn't have all of the money. I asked the sweet bail bondsman if I could pay her fourteen hundred dollars. She agreed to put me on a payment plan. When she gave me my receipt, I felt like I had Willy Wonka's golden ticket in hand. She told me that his bail would be posted within the hour, and Ruben would be released around midnight.

When I got home, I stayed up with my phone in my hand. I was anxious for Ruben's call. I couldn't wait to see him.

As I dozed off, my phone rang.

"Hello, bae? They are about to let me go. So you can be on your way."

I jumped out of bed, grabbed my keys, and sped to the jail. I was so happy to see that man. It was the first night that I rested while I slept since he'd been gone.

The following day, Ruben and I had a conversation about jobs. His brother told him that he could put in a good word with his manager at the restaurant to get Ruben a job. Ruben and I dropped his brother off at work, and Ruben accompanied him inside the restaurant to speak with the manager. I waited in the car for Ruben to return. When he did, he said that the manager hired him on the spot, and he was to come back the next day for orientation. The only problem was that Ruben needed a white shirt and black shoes. I told Ruben that I would purchase the items for him. As I drove to the store, I told Ruben my expectations. I explained that he would be responsible for the remaining portion of his bail and half of the rent. I detected a slight attitude, but Ruben agreed to my terms.

As time went on, I noticed that Ruben's case wasn't handled correctly. His court-appointed lawyer didn't seem to know who Ruben was. In addition, his caseload was backed up. So, I decided to call the sweet bail bondsman and ask her if she knew of a good lawyer for a reasonable price. She recommended an attorney, and I contacted him right away.

The lawyer agreed to start on Ruben's case for fourteen hundred dollars. The total was forty-five hundred dollars. The attorney allowed me to pay the remaining balance in installments. I didn't have the required fourteen hundred, so I decided to use the title of my car to get a fourteen hundred dollar loan. I paid the attorney and felt good that he was the right man for the job.

As soon as I let my guard down with Ruben, things started to shift. I found text messages on his phone from other women. He had made plans to meet up with one of the women. He lied and told me that the women were his cousin. I saw red, and before I knew what was happening, I balled my hand into a fist and punched him in the face. This wasn't the first time that Ruben had disrespected me. Before he went to jail, there were arguments about flirtatious messages that I found on his phone. I believed that infidelity was behind us. I was wrong.

Things went from bad to worse. Three months later, Ruben quit his job at the restaurant. When I asked him why he quit, he told me someone had said something racist to him. I asked him what his plan was. He shrugged his shoulders and said to me that he would get another job. I can't say that I believed him. Ruben's bum behavior got ridiculous in a short amount of time. He started hanging out more in my car and showing off the material possessions that I worked hard to get. He even went as far as to tell people that my car was a car that he purchased for me.

Whenever he got mad, he threatened me and my family. When Ruben drank and took ecstasy pills, he would put his hands on me. He loved to tell people that he was a Muslim, but he didn't follow the religion as he should've. It was as if it were a trend.

I humbled myself and called the bail bondsman. I asked her if I could pay her fifty-dollar installments because Ruben lost his job. To my relief, she agreed. Next, I called the lawyer and pleaded with him not to drop Ruben's case. I was thankful that he decided to let me pay what I could as long as I contacted him.

After overcoming those hurdles, I fought with the man I was fighting so hard for. Ruben would drop me off at work to go out to look for a job. But, he was always hanging out with his cousin at his cousin's home. Ruben argued that I was nagging whenever I asked him about finding employment. I was fed up.

Chapter Five

"Sometimes, your rejection from men is your protection from God." - Pastor R.C. Blakes

J ust as I was at my wit's end, I received a call that shook me to my core. There was something different in my aunt's voice when I answered her call. My spine curved in preparation for what the phone call was about.

"Your dad's in ICU," she said.

The phone nearly slipped from my palm. I immediately hit the blinker signal in my car and headed toward the hospital. The tears streamed down my face as I thought of how special my dad was to me. My brain overflowed with thoughts of us fishing, cooking together, or just enjoying our time with each other. Before I knew it, I was in the hospital parking lot. I swerved into a parking spot and threw the gear shift to park. As I hopped out of the car, I noticed I was well over the bright white line, but there was no time to straighten my car. In my head, I said an apology to whoever attempted to park in the spot next to me. Then, I darted across the street to the hospital entrance. I ran across the street as traffic flowed. Cars honked at me, but my only thought was getting to my dad. When I made it to the hospital's fifth floor, I was winded. I quickly tried to adjust my clothing and wiped the tears from my face before entering his room. As soon as I opened the door, my dad turned and smiled at me. He was so happy to see me, and I was elated to see him.

"Dad, are you okay?"

He responded, "Yes, daughter. I'm good. I'm ready to get out of here."

I told him that I wanted the same.

We sat around and talked for hours before the doctor came into the room. He asked if he could speak to the family, and we all gathered around to hear what he had to say. He held an x-ray toward the light to give us a clearer view of the findings on my dad's brain. The doctor explained that my father had been having strokes in his sleep, and to solve the problem, the best decision would be to place a trach in his neck.

I walked away and immediately called my mom. She'd gone to nursing school before deciding to pursue teaching. I knew that she would have some insight. After explaining what I'd been told, my mom asked to speak with the doctor. My mother and father were no longer together, but there was no bitterness between them. Instead, they did what they had to do to co-parent effectively.

I shouted down the corridor to the doctor and explained that my mother would like to speak with him.

"Yes, ma'am. Be right there," he replied.

Even though his words were pleasant, it was the way he spoke that wholly turned my family and me off. There was an underlying attitude, and he made us feel as if we were bothering him.

"Hello. I'd like to know the reason Rickey Moore needs a

trach in his neck. I know others that have had strokes and don't have to be treated with such extreme measures."

My mom listened as the doctor repeated the exact words he'd told us. When the doctor passed the phone back to me, he exited the room before I lifted it to my ear. The first thing my mom told me was not to let them do the procedure.

"I don't think it's necessary. Once he has the trach, he'll have to go to rehab and be limited by so much," my mom revealed.

She then asked that I let her speak with my aunt and father. She told them the same. We agreed and said that we wouldn't consent to the procedure. I don't think my dad completely understood what was happening. He seemed normal, but his brain had been affected.

It wasn't long before the doctor returned with paperwork to sign for the trach in my father's neck. We didn't read nor sign the papers presented. My grandmother, aunt, and I explained that we would go to the hospital cafeteria to grab a bite to eat as my dad rested. We asked that nothing be decided or finalized until we returned. The doctor said that it was no problem and would wait for us to return.

We were gone no more than an hour. When we returned, the first thing we noticed was that the curtain in my dad's room was pulled closed. I snatched the curtain back to see that my father and the hospital bed were gone.

"NURSE," I shouted.

My aunt went to the hallway to see if she could find the nearest nurse. When she spotted a young nurse in the hallway, she asked where Rickey Moore was. The nurse's response echoed in my ears.

"He's been brought down for his trach procedure."

"You're telling me that my father is having major surgery without our permission or our knowledge. The doctor said that he would wait for us to come back before making a decision.

The nurse didn't want any part of giving us any more information. Instead, she explained that the next doctor, on-call, should arrive in an hour or so and that we could speak with him. I felt my knees weaken. In an instant, my grandmother, aunt, and I had a face full of tears.

Through tears, my aunt voiced to the nurse, "Why would y'all take advantage of my brother. He had a stroke. He's not in his right mind."

My dad wanted to get home and out of the hospital as quickly as possible. Those were his words before having a trach placed in his neck. Eight months passed before we were able to get my dad home. Before the trach was placed in my dad's neck, he talked like he always had. After the trach placement, he slurred his words. My dad started to lose his hair, and he kept fluid on his legs and feet, which caused them to swell like balloons. It's the most horrible thing I've ever had to see. We felt that he needed to be compensated for all the suffering my dad was enduring. We contacted a lawyer, but nothing could be done due to my dad signing the consent.

Things seemed to be getting as back to normal as they could. My dad called and asked if he could take me to dinner as an early birthday celebration close to my birthday. We laughed and joked over the dinner. We had such a fantastic time.

The summer heat came, and my dad seemed to be doing better. He called me one humid day and asked that I take him to Walmart when I got off work to purchase a few things. I told him that I had no problem bringing him and was scheduled to get off work at eight o'clock. He asked that I pick him up from my grandmother's house, and I agreed.

It was usual for me to text my dad throughout the day. So when he stopped responding around noon, I figured he was taking a nap. I texted him again before I left work, but there was no response again. So I just thought that he was still napping and decided to pick Ruben up from his cousin's house before running errands with my dad.

As I drove, my aunt called. Her voice was heavy with solemn.

"Alyssa? I need you to come to the hospital NOW."

I didn't respond to her. The phone fell to my lap. I made a u-turn and started driving 90 miles per hour on the street, weaving between cars. I parked my car and ran inside the emergency room in a panic. A hospital worker asked who I was, and I explained that I was Rickey Moore's daughter. The worker told me the room number, and I darted by the nurses' station. I burst open the door and saw my family circled a bed. Some were crying. I noticed a white sheet and feet that were uncovered.

There was instant nausea in my stomach.

"What's going on?"

My aunt released through cries, "Your dad is gone."

I ran out of the room, not wanting to accept what I'd just been told. I found the closest space and retreated. I didn't want to be around anyone. I didn't want the moment to be real.

Wailing and crying in an empty room, my aunt pushed the door open.

"Why did he have to go? What did I do wrong?"

The hospital staff entered and tried to console me. I felt triggered.

I yelled at them, "You'll killed my dad. He didn't need a damn trach in his throat. Just leave me alone."

My heart was broken into even more pieces when I learned from my grandmother that my four-year-old cousin found my dad in the bathroom. He was found in the bathtub on his back. He'd slipped bumped his head, and the trach went down his throat.

Days after, I couldn't eat; I was thoroughly checked out half the time. People would be talking to me, and I had no idea what they were saying. I was almost numb. My dad and I never had the chance to celebrate my birthday on my actual birthday. Instead, I basked in the memory of him taking me out to dinner as an early birthday celebration. I'm grateful for that moment that we shared.

My dad's funeral was four days after my twenty-second birthday. I needed support to get through the day. Ruben refused to attend my father's funeral with me because he stated that he didn't like funerals. Who liked funerals? I needed his support, and he made it very clear that all that I was going through was not a priority for him.

One of the last lessons my dad gave me was never to be an option for a man and never to let a man show me more than once that he doesn't care. So after the funeral, I told Ruben to pack his stuff. I was done. Ruben refused to leave, so I had to get the law involved.

We lived in a predominantly Caucasian area, and it seemed like the entire police department pulled up. A friendly officer, Deputy Perkins, asked about the situation and then told Ruben to pack his belongings to leave. The officer informed me that I would have to get a Peace Order to protect me from Ruben coming around. The deputy also gave me sound advice, much like my dad. Deputy Perkins said, "Never let a man stay in your home for free, never let a man put his hands on you, and never let a man show you're then once that he doesn't care about you."

When the coast was clear of Ruben and the heavy police presence, his brother came out of the room. I'd forgotten that he was even there.

ALYSSA MOORE

"Sis, that's my brother, but I told him that you were gonna get fed up with him not helping out. Honestly, I was fed up with you two arguing. You had every right to put him out. Nothing is free. There aren't many women that would do all that you've done for him."

My head throbbed, and I was over the entire day. He had no clue that frustration was far past Ruben not helping out. I didn't have the energy to explain my stance. I just needed a minute to be still.

It'd been a few days since I'd put Ruben out. I knew that he had a court date approaching. I was already heavily tied into his case. I also still cared about him. He'd done everything for me to not give a damn about him, but I have a big heart. As soon as I stepped inside the courtroom, Ruben sat next to me. He began to shred his lawyer to pieces.

"What's taking Mr. Benny so long to get this case dropped," he argued.

He disgusted me. I spewed, "First of all, you are a felon. You will continue to have court dates. You should be grateful that he even took your case. He's done more for you than any court-appointed lawyer has done in the past."

I rolled my eyes and scooted a few inches away from him. It was at that moment that I regretted showing up.

When the judge called Ruben, he approached the bench with aggression. He told the judge that he was firing Mr. Benny. I couldn't believe what I was hearing. I wanted to shout at him inside of the court. But, it was best that I just exited the courtroom. I met Mr. Benny outside the courtroom doors and apologized. I begged him to continue to work on Ruben's case. As usual, I made excuses for Ruben. I told Mr. Benny that he was just upset that things weren't moving as fast as he liked.

"I'm sorry, Miss Moore. I can't overrule the decision that he made. Especially since he did so in front of a judge."

At that moment, I realized how embarrassing it must have been for Mr. Benny to be called out in front of a judge. I felt even worse.

Mr. Benny continued, "Again, I do apologize, Miss Moore. It's nothing personal. But, what's done is done. His files will be returned to the state."

How could Ruben make a decision about my money? I was almost finished paying Mr. Benny, and he fired him with no good reason why. I cried as I watched Mr. Benny walk away. Ruben had flushed my money down the toilet. I saw red. I was beyond angry. I didn't want to see Ruben or talk to him.

By the time I drove away from the courthouse, I had thirty missed calls from Ruben. I had nothing to say to him. When I noticed an incoming call from Mr. Benny, I answered right away.

Mr. Benny told me how he'd been receiving threatening phone calls from Ruben. Ruben wanted what had been paid to Mr. Benny refunded to him, or he would sue him. Ruben wanted the money I had spent on his behalf to Mr. Benny. I apologized again and told him that I would contact Ruben to stop.

"WHY ARE YOU CALLING THAT MAN AND THREATENING HIM? That's not even your money. IT'S MY MONEY. You fired him. He doesn't owe you ANYTHING," I yelled into my cellphone. I hung up before Ruben responded.

I just wanted to be done with him.

Chapter Six

"If you continuously have negative people who don't mean you any good in your circle, you will not get things accomplished in life. You will always get backfired because they are in the midst of your accomplishments." - Pastor R.C. Blakes

Months after my dad's passing, I knew I needed to change my life. I needed a fresh start. It'd been a year and a half since Ruben and I ended. I felt relief. I was no longer living in stress and had finally caught up and paid off my debt because of Ruben. I'd always had my sight set on moving to Houston. Something was telling me that the time was now. I'd saved my money and was ready for a new chapter. After a girl's trip to Atlanta, I decided to put my plan in motion.

Ruben's brother and I were still living together. He wasn't a bad roommate. I never had an issue with him and money. He regularly helped with rent and bills. Some days, we'd even go out to get daiquiris.

When I got back, I talked with him. I explained that I would be moving to Houston in the new year, and he's more than welcome to come. I knew that he had a brother and sister who lived in Houston. So I figured he could live with them until he got on his feet in a new city. He welcomed the change and said that he would start looking for jobs in Houston.

The next day, I got online and started researching apartments. I found some apartments that I liked and called to inquire about the application. I was worried about my credit affecting an approval. The apartment manager informed me that I would be instantly approved if I paid the last two months and the first month's rent. I'd saved up a lot of cash and was so excited to do something for myself with it.

In my excitement, I did what most of us do. I posted my exciting news on social media. But, forgetting that Ruben and I were still friends on social media, I didn't realize that he would see my post.

Within minutes of the phone being on my feed, I received a text from Ruben. He wanted to know when I was moving to Houston and if he could come with his brother and me. He said that the job opportunities were much better in Houston. But, the Ruben that I knew was never interested in getting a job.

I told him that he could ride with me to Houston, but I would drop him and his brother by their relatives. He couldn't stay with me. Ruben agreed but never thanked me for the opportunity. I noticed it, and it didn't sit right with me. Something in my gut told me that he would do something spiteful to stop his brother from moving to Houston.

A few days went by, while at work, I received back-to-back calls from Ruben's brother. Then, when I went to lunch and returned his call, he didn't say hello.

"MAN, WHAT'S GOING ON BETWEEN YOU AND MY BROTHER?"

ALYSSA MOORE

I was taken aback by his question. It'd been days since Ruben, and I spoke, and our conversation wasn't volatile.

He continued, "I'm tired of you and my brother with the bullshit. I told you'll to keep me out of it. He just told me that you called the police on him, and now he's on a high-speed chase."

Baffled, I responded with logic, "Why would I need to call the police on him? He doesn't even have a car. How is he on a high-speed chase? Look, my lunch break is over. Believe what you want."

When I hung up on him, I sent a text message. I told him to pack his belongings and find somewhere to stay. I also asked that he be gone by the time I got home. I didn't want the drama.

He knew how much of a pathological liar Ruben was. This was no different.

When I texted him that I would be going to Houston alone, he immediately responded and asked why. I didn't feel the need to explain. There were multiple texts of apologies, but my mind was made up. He allowed Ruben to mess up what could've been a great opportunity.

Chapter Seven

"You gonna have to leave your life available long enough for a king to come around." - Pastor R.C. Blakes

As 2021 began, I was ready to embark on a new journey. I woke up the morning I was set to arrive in Houston and enjoyed the simple things I knew I would miss. I listened as my grandmother and mom laughed and the giggles of my little sister. I packed last-minute items and enjoyed little moments with my grandmother, grandfather, mom, and little sister.

My grandfather taught me a lot about men. He always told me never let a man stay in your place rent-free, let a man win you, and you don't have to ask a man for anything; it's just going to happen randomly. We still have our little talks, and I cherish them.

No matter how old I may get, my grandfather always tells me to let him know if I need anything. I wouldn't dare ask my grandparents for anything. They've done so much for me.

I have the spirit of a hustler. Even if I am to my last dollar, I will get a second job or deliver food or groceries. So there's a lot of hustle in me.

They planned to ride with me to Houston to get set up in my new space. Things were lined up. I had a new apartment, and I knew that I would easily find a job. When I delivered packages, I met a lovely older lady who started a conversation with me. I told her how excited I was to move to Houston. She told me that her niece was a manager for the same company in Houston. I was elated to take the woman's information.

My family and I arrived in Houston that evening. I was not prepared for how massive and many interstates there were. We missed an exit and had to drive an additional ten minutes to take the next exit. Houston interstates have left and right exits. I was only used to exiting to the right in New Orleans. There were many shocks as I adjusted to my new life, but I was ready for them.

I contacted the lady's niece as soon as I got to Houston. She informed me where to go online to complete an application and submit information for a background check. However, I didn't know how long it would take for my background information to come back. So, I decided to find a job through a temp service. It didn't take long before I was put on the schedule at the delivery company. It was a cool job, but I wanted more.

I'd purchased my Transportation Worker Identification Credential in New Orleans because it was a goal to work in chemical plants. I knew many people who made a good living working in chemical plants. But, I needed more certifications before I could get into the field. I took all of the required tests and passed each one. It wasn't until I had one foot in the door that I realized that working in the field wasn't for me. I needed something more permanent than a contracting position. So, I continued to work in the plant while I applied for other jobs on career websites. I went through a tedious interview process and finally received the job of my dreams at a Fortune 500 company. I now have a 401K and excellent benefits.

Just when I thought it was all over, Ruben slithered back into the picture. This time, uninvitedly. When we were together, Ruben allowed me to carry him and his brother on my taxes. There was no issue. Ruben accompanied me to the tax office and presented the preparer with all his information. I gave him and his brother one thousand dollars each. Many people told me not to give him anything.

So, when I received a letter from the IRS saying that I was being audited, my heart sank. I went into a sweat and needed a seat to finish reading the letter. I immediately grabbed my phone and called the contact number on the government letter. After impatiently holding, a representative informed me that Ruben called and stated that I was not obligated to carry him on my taxes. Ruben reached a new low. I wasn't bothering him. Why did he feel the need to mess with me and my finances? I was so angry that I called him as soon as I ended the call with the IRS. As soon as I asked him about it, he denied everything.

"Man, I didn't do that shit. Alyssa, why would I do that? I don't care how mad we are at each other; I wouldn't do you like that. I'm not low down and dirty like that."

Ruben is the poster child for low down and dirty. I didn't believe a word he said.

I hung up on him and started to figure out what was the best thing for me to do. I went into my tax office and explained the situation to the preparer. She helped me by sending the necessary information over to the IRS. It took almost a month for me to have my audit overturned.

I don't wish any bad on Ruben. However, I'm also fully aware that karma is a bitch.

I'm so grateful for everything God has done for me. I have

a job that I love and want to retire from. I also have been single for three years. I needed some time to find out what I like and enjoy about myself. I'm constantly learning new things about myself without the distractions of a man. The time has been good for me. I now know what my red flags and deal breakers are. I know how I should be treated, and I refuse to accept anything less.

Epilogue

I was raised in the church. I don't remember when I wasn't in the church choir. It seems as if as soon as my sister and I could talk, my grandmother had us in the choir stand. She would say, "You are going to sing and praise the Lord." Some of my fondest memories are singing soprano or the excitement of having a solo.

I allowed my relationships with men to get between my relationship with God. I stopped going to church and lacked in areas I shouldn't have, like prayer and worship. It's no one's fault but my own. I recognized my faults and acknowledged them. I'd been a servant to so many people who only trampled over me. I was loyal to those that were the most disloyal to me. I'd been hurt and covered my pain or pretended that somehow, I was the cause of my hurt. As I healed, I vowed to start putting myself first. It was time to work on me.

I sat in my living room listening to R.C. Blakes preach a sermon one morning. The sermon was about one of his books. Pastor Blakes touched me as he spoke of women should not feel as if they have to buy love because we are queens. He said that queens set standards for themselves. Men will only do what you allow them to do. In that moment, I realized that it was time to put Alyssa first. I had to begin to do my self work.

I decided to look up my credit. It had been so long since I had. Honestly, I was afraid of what I might see. But I did, and to say I was disappointed would be an understatement.

"How am I going to get this up," I mumbled to myself.

Instantly, my mother's words replayed in my head. "Never pay someone to do something for you that you could do for yourself."

It was then that I decided that I messed it up and I would clean up my mess.

On my next day off, I purchased a notebook. I wrote down all of the collections on my credit report. The next day, I started calling the creditors and negotiating payments. I paid off six creditors. Whenever I received a paid in full letter in the mail or via email, I jumped for joy. I was finally putting myself first, and it felt good.

One day, a friend and I discussed our future goals. Both of us had a goal of purchasing a home. Intrigued with our conversation, I looked at my credit score to find that it had jumped nearly fifty points. I cried tears of joy.

As women, we go through so much. There isn't a manual of dos and don'ts. We all have made mistakes, and none of us are above making future mistakes. Low self-esteem doesn't have an age limit. Men manipulate at all ages. I hope my experiences in this book have encouraged a woman to keep going. No man will make you happy if you aren't first happy with yourself. The first person we should fall in love with is ourselves. Then, we can share it with others.

My temper could've landed me in jail. No man is worth my freedom. I've learned so many lessons in just twenty-four years. First, I will never beg a man to be with me, ever again. There isn't a penis that powerful. Second, I will never be okay with a man calling me out of my name. It's disrespectful, and I will never tolerate it again. Third, any man I have a relationship with in the future will provide for himself. I want a man, not a child that I will have to provide for. Lastly, I will never have a man who only cares about what I can do for him or what I have. I desire a man who will do things without me having to ask, a man who takes the initiative.

Thank you all for reading my book. I pray that every woman who has read these pages never settles for less than she deserves. Don't ever give up on God because God will never give up on you.

About the Author

As a young girl growing up in New Orleans, LA, I overcame many trials and tribulations. My mom and grandparents always told me that I should write a book because of the tremendous amount of growth they've witnessed in me. I hope that my words and obstacles can help young women on their journey in womanhood. Unfortunately, womanhood doesn't come with a manual. This book is intended to motivate young women with a lack of self-esteem that they don't need a man to validate who they are. Before any man could value me, I had to learn to love myself.

I've learned from my experiences, and I now know my worth. Thank you for reading my story. I hope these words resonate with you and help young women learn to love and prioritize themselves.

Made in the USA
Middletown, DE
22 September 2022